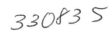

JASON PORTERFIELD

ROSEN
PUBLISHING

NEW YORK

Published in 2016 by The Rosen Publishing Group, Inc.
29 East 21st Street, New York, NY 10010

First Edition

Library of Congress Cataloging-in-Publication Data
Porterfield, Jason, author.
 Tim Berners-Lee / Jason Porterfield. -- First Edition.
    pages cm. -- (Tech pioneers)
 Includes bibliographical references and index.
 ISBN 978-1-4994-6290-6 (library bound)
 1. Berners-Lee, Tim--Juvenile literature. 2. Telecommunications engi-
neers--Great Britain--Biography--Juvenile literature. 3. Computer sci-
entists--Great Britain--Biography--Juvenile literature. 4. World Wide
Web--History--Juvenile literature. I. Title.
 TK5102.56.B47P67 2015
 004.67'8092--dc23

                                                                2015033181

Manufactured in the United States of America

CONTENTS

INTRODUCTION

The opening ceremony of the 2012 Summer Olympic Games in London, England, included all of the glamour and spectacle usually associated with such global events. The entertainment featured such well-known figures as Queen Elizabeth II, soccer star David Beckham, and fictional spy James Bond.

At the heart of the ceremony was a man named Tim Berners-Lee, whose work in the 1980s and early 1990s led to the invention of the World Wide Web. Stationed at a vintage NeXT computer similar to the one he used to write the program, he used Twitter to send out the message, "This is for everyone." The same message was then spelled out in lights around the stadium, referring to both the Olympic games and the World Wide Web. The

Tim Berners-Lee appears at the opening ceremony for the 2012 Summer Olympics, alongside a computer similar to the one he used to invent the World Wide Web.

audience cheered, even as some television hosts admitted they had never heard of him.

Berners-Lee's part in the opening ceremony represents the quiet determination that led to his invention. A mathematics and electronics enthusiast from an early age, he spent several years working for electronics firms. During a brief stint working at one of the world's leading physics research facilities, he developed a computer program that would eventually become the World Wide Web. Realizing that his program had the potential to dramatically change the way people communicate, he continued to work on it even when he couldn't get official support. After he got that support, he put together a team of very capable computer scientists to help make the World Wide Web a reality. To get the Web going, Berners-Lee himself had to invent new programming languages and applications that had their basis in early network technology.

Before the World Wide Web came into being, there was no way to go online to listen to music, watch a video, check the latest sports scores, or get up-to-the minute international news. Today, people use the Web for everything from sending e-mail and paying bills to turning in work or school assignments. Social media websites help people stay in touch over long distances, and commerce sites let shoppers buy things without having to go into a store. The World Wide Web has become a place where people can share photos, write about their experiences, and even make new friends.

Berners-Lee did not imagine most of those things happening after his invention went live in 1990. It was designed with research and academics in mind, but he quickly saw his invention's potential. He has greeted the growth of the Web enthusiastically and with the hope that it can be used to help more people. In the years after the World Wide Web first went online, he has worked tirelessly to make sure that it remains open to all users and to make it available in places where Web service was once impossible. In his work with the World Wide Web Consortium and other groups, he continues to strive for a Web that truly is for everyone.

Chapter One

GROWING UP WIRED

Power
Control

What was the Bab

Timothy John Berners-Lee was born on June 8, 1955, in London, England. His parents were both pioneers in computing, though they had come to computer science from different fields.

His mother, Mary Lee Woods, was born in 1924. She studied mathematics at the University of Birmingham during World War II. She contributed to the United Kingdom's war effort by serving a two-year fellowship at an aeronautical research facility in Farnborough and then for the Telecommunications Research Establishment at

Melvern until 1946, when she left to finish her degree. She then spent four years pursuing an astrophysics fellowship at the Mount Stromlo Observatory in Canberra, Australia, before returning home in 1951. She took a job at the electronics firm Ferranti in Manchester, where she worked as a computer engineer on a team lead by pioneering computer scientist John Bennett.

Bennett's task was to develop a computer for Manchester University and transform it into a machine that

The Manchester Mark I was the first computer built that was capable of storing program information in an electronic memory system.

could be sold on the commercial market. Customers for this modified Manchester Computer would include universities, research facilities, and government agencies. They developed the Ferranti Mark I and Mark I Star computers in 1951. Mary Lee Woods worked as a programmer for both machines.

Mary Lee Woods eventually became colleagues with a mathematician and electrical engineer named Conway Berners-Lee. Born in 1921, he had tried to volunteer for military service at the outbreak of World War II. Instead, he was redirected by the United Kingdom's government into a program for people skilled in math and attended the University of Cambridge's Trinity College in 1940.

Conway graduated with a degree in mathematics as part of a compressed two-year course of study. After finishing his degree, he learned electrical engineering and was able to join the British army as a member of the Corps of Royal Electrical and Mechanical Engineers. He worked on searchlight radar and gun laying in England. After the war, the army stationed him in Egypt, where he joined the statistics bureau in Cairo. One of the projects he worked on involved closing down a record-keeping system that relied on punched cards to keep track of army personnel and equipment. He left the army in 1947 with the rank of major. He returned to England and was hired by Imperial Chemical Industries to work on a punch card data processing system.

FROM BABBAGE TO FERRANTI

Ferranti was a leader in the development of early computers. Mechanical devices designed to help people make calculations and automate some machines had been around for centuries. British inventor Charles Babbage (1791–1871) designed two early programmable computers, called the Difference Engine and the Analytical Engine, in the mid-nineteenth century. His designs used punched cards to input data, and the machines would have provided responses using a printer, a curve plotter, and a bell. Neither was built in his lifetime, though the punch card system was used in computing well into the twentieth century.

Computers that used electrical circuits and a branch of mathematics called Boolean algebra to perform digital computations were created in the 1930s. The first programmable electronic digital computers were built in the 1940s. The microchip and microprocessor had not been invented, and these machines took up rooms of space just to hold all of the electronic relays, switches, and cooling devices they needed.

Mary Lee Woods and Conway Berners-Lee first met in 1952 at Ferranti's annual Christmas party. He joined the company at its London office in 1953, and he and Mary Lee Woods began dating after she transferred to the same office. They were married in 1954 and settled down in southwest London. Mary continued working at Ferranti until May 1955, leaving the company for Tim's birth.

PRECOCIOUS CHILDHOOD

When he was a very small child, Tim's parents took him to see where Conway worked and showed him one of the early Ferranti computers. He thought it looked like a big cabinet that had a clock on it and with a desk with a paper tape reader and punch alongside it. After the family returned home, Tim created his own "computer" by

Ferranti was a developer and manufacturer of several key technological breakthroughs related to England's defense industry, including systems designed to track aircraft.

putting a clock in a cabinet, pushing a desk against it, and using cardboard boxes for the paper tape feeds.

Imagination, science, and exploration played a big role in the childhoods of Tim and his three younger siblings. They were encouraged to follow their interests. Mary and Conway Berners-Lee were both raised by parents who had progressive ideas about the role of women in society. Mary was encouraged to apply herself in the fields that interested her, even at a time when young women weren't encouraged to study mathematics. Even after Tim and his three siblings were born, she continued to take on computer science projects that she found interesting, though it was unusual at that time for women to work after they had children. She did the programming work at home in her spare time. She also became a math teacher. Conway continued working at Ferranti, where he worked on projects that included techniques for sorting and dating files and a way to compress text to save memory space. He stayed at Ferranti through several mergers before retiring in 1986.

Like his parents, Tim was interested in math and was talented in working with numbers. Mary and Conway Berners-Lee encouraged their children to see math as fun but also to take it seriously. In a 2001 *Time* magazine story, Tim recalled teasing his younger brother—who was in grade school at the time—for not knowing the square root of negative four.

Tim attended Sheen Mount Primary School, where he quickly realized that he wasn't very good at sports. However, he had two close friends who shared his love of science. During recess, the boys would walk around their school's playground and talk about physics, biology, and other science subjects. They even talked about writing a book about science, but they were sidetracked by trying to build an underground laboratory where Tim would be in charge of writing it. They also attempted to make their own electromagnets out of nails and wire but never succeeded.

Children in England start their high school education earlier than in the United States, and when he turned eleven, Tim's parents enrolled him at Emanuel School in southwest London. Emanuel was an all-boys school at that time, but it had a very strong reputation as a place of learning. The school was located between two railroad tracks, which Berners-Lee would later remember in an Academy of Achievement interview made it "very difficult to escape from." Many of the kids there took up a hobby called train spotting. They would watch for trains to go by and keep records on each one that passed. Tim happily joined them. He kept a model railway in his room and soon started making electrical gadgets to control his locomotives.

Athletics were a big part of life at the school, but Tim still preferred hiking and being outdoors to playing sports that involved throwing or catching balls. Tim made friends easily, and he and the other boys often spent weekends and vacations together hiking through the countryside outside the city. He also found that he liked rowing, both the physical work of pulling the oars and the feeling of being on the water.

He continued tinkering with electronics and became interested in books. The Berners-Lee family didn't own a television, and Tim's parents encouraged their children to read. Tim liked mysteries, such as those by Agatha Christie. He became particularly interested in science fiction and would sometimes stay up all night to finish reading a novel. His favorite authors included the science fiction writers John Wyndham and Arthur C. Clarke. Tim would one day use Clarke's short story "Dial F for Frankenstein" to explain how the World Wide Web worked. In the story, computers become so interconnected that they eventually take on a life of their own.

In addition to the support he received from his parents, many of Tim's teachers at school encouraged his interests. A math teacher and a chemistry teacher were particularly easy for him to approach because of their enthusiasm for the subjects they taught.

OFF TO UNIVERSITY

Tim finished his high school education at Emanuel School in 1973 with excellent grades, particularly in math and science. He applied to study at the University of Oxford and was accepted into the school's famous Queen's College. Berners-Lee enjoyed being on his

Queen's College at the University of Oxford was founded in 1341 and named in honor of Queen Philippa of Hainault, the wife of King Edward III.

own and settled into university life. Oxford is the oldest English-speaking university in the world, and he appreciated its history. He decided to study physics because he considered it a middle ground between math and electronics. He would be able to use it in a science-related career. Though he started studying physics for practical reasons, he quickly became fascinated by the subject. His fellow students and his professors recognized his brilliance and his abilities. He applied himself and was able to graduate in 1976 with high honors.

He also spent time in the outdoors. Tim had always enjoyed going for walks and hiking, and he led an active lifestyle. If he was having trouble working out a physics problem for class, he would take time out from his studies to go boating or go out into the countryside. He

Mainframe computers available in the 1970s, such as the example shown here, needed a large amount of space for all of their components.

worked at a sawmill during the summer so that he could save up for ski trips to the European mainland.

Tim also made room for his love of electronics and inventing. He also had his first chances to actually use computers similar to those that his parents

built. However, he and a friend decided to hack into the mainframe computer used by Oxford's nuclear physics laboratory without permission. When they were caught, Berners-Lee was banned from using it for the rest of his time at college.

He decided to build his own computer and bought a used television set from a shop down the street from his apartment. Berners-Lee utilized a soldering iron to construct a working computer out of the television, a calculator that he had salvaged from a dumpster, and a battery from a car. He also started writing his own computer programming languages.

He enjoyed working with computers and he understood how they operated at a time when such knowledge was fairly rare. He understood how their components worked together and communicated. Today, he would easily be able to get a second college degree in computer science. However, not many colleges and universities had computer science departments at that time. Most of the few that did were located in the United States, and Berners-Lee was unaware of those opportunities. Fortunately, he found his skills to be in high demand in the private sector.

Chapter Two

From Telecoms to Physics

Tim Berners-Lee had a varied career in the years leading up to his work at CERN, with most of his work focusing on writing software and solving design and usability problems. He was able to translate his passion for electronics and his interest in computers into many different roles.

The Engineering Life

At the time that Berners-Lee graduated from Oxford, it was common for British companies to come onto university campuses and recruit students who were about to graduate. One of those firms was a communications equipment manufacturer called Plessey Telecommunications based in the town of Poole, in the county of Dorset

A woman assembles circuit boards for Plessey in 1958. Plessey was a leader in radio technology and expanded into other forms of electronic communication in the 1950s.

along the southern coast of England. He thought the company's electrical engineering jobs sounded interesting, and he liked the idea of working in a seaside town.

His girlfriend at the time, Jane Northcote, also accepted a job offer from Plessey. The pay was not great and there weren't many opportunities to advance within the company, but they were popular in Plessey's small social scene. Both enjoyed hiking, and Dorset provided plenty of opportunities to explore the countryside.

Berners-Lee and Northcote met at Oxford and began dating while both were still attending college. The couple shared interests in the outdoors and computer science. Northcote studied nuclear physics and graduated with honors in 1976. The two married soon after going to work at Plessey, though the marriage ended in divorce just a couple years later. Berners-Lee doesn't often talk about his family and personal life, and does not discuss his first marriage. Northcote herself has made

Microchips can transmit the energy to control the processes and functions needed for a computer to run. They replaced the bulky equipment used to run early computers.

many significant contributions to the field of computer science, including her work on developing silicon microchips.

Berners-Lee was employed in the mathematics lab of the company's controls division, and his coworkers quickly recognized his brilliance and his down-to-earth manner. He helped develop early barcode technology and worked on message relay and distributed transaction systems, both of which were electrical components that Plessey manufactured for private companies.

Tim left Plessey in 1978 and went to work for D. G. Nash in Ferndown, another town in Dorset. The company's owners, Dennis Nash and John Poole, were trying to develop typesetting software for automated printing equipment. Tim's software allowed people to program instructions into the printing systems so that they could go through their processes on their own. He also helped build multitasking operating systems for the typesetting process.

THE CONSULTANT

Berners-Lee left D. G. Nash in 1979 and became an independent consultant. The field of computer science was expanding rapidly at that time as the technology advanced. Improvements to microchips allowed for more data to be stored, and other elements that made it easier to exchange information had been developed. Computers were being used in more ways than ever, and more and more different types of machines were being developed. They were also getting smaller and less expensive, making them more widely available to businesses and organizations that might not have had room for them or enough money to afford them. Universities, governments, and private companies were all looking for ways to get the most out of their computers. People like Berners-Lee were in high demand because of their ability to find better ways to organize data and systems.

In June 1980, Berners-Lee and his friend Kevin Rogers were hired as consultants for the European Organization for Nuclear Research (CERN). Located on the border of Switzerland and France near the Swiss city of Geneva, CERN is one of the world's leading physics research centers. Scientists and engineers from around the world go to CERN to study matter and how it behaves. The center is famous for its particle accelerators, which are machines that blast nuclear particles through a series of tubes located in a large underground tunnel. The particles smash into each other at high speeds and sometimes create new particles. By recording these collisions and their results, scientists can gain a better understanding of how atoms are constructed and behave.

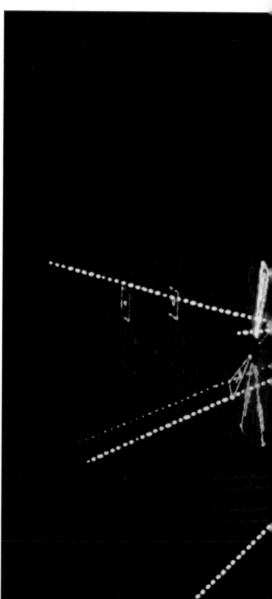

The work done at CERN is very expensive, and governments usually work together on experiments. They have to be able to share information with each other, and their data has to be readable on CERN's computers as well as their computers back home. The center didn't have a good way to share data when Berners-Lee was hired to work there in 1980. Researchers brought a

Researchers at CERN found a new particle in 1982 using the UA1 detector, part of the supercollider that monitors the properties of particles.

variety of machines and software with them to do their work. Today, most computers, smartphones, and tablets run on operating systems that can communicate with one another fairly easily. That wasn't the case in 1980, when many computers simply weren't compatible.

When Berners-Lee was hired, CERN was working on replacing the control system that ran two of the center's particle accelerators. He and the other consultants had to build software that could work within a very large system and interact with a variety of machines, computer hardware, and other programs. Daily meetings between team members were key to knowing what everyone was working on, and Berners-Lee had trouble remembering names and faces. He decided to write a program that he could use to keep track of these associations so that he could keep all of the software projects organized.

Most computer programs stored information in a hierarchical way—often called a tree structure—in which information flowed from a common "root" and "trunk" branching off into separate subcategories, which might yield other subcategories. Everything went into a category and each category had a clear order, ranked from highest to lowest. One could find information only by going up or down the tree, not by cutting across.

Berners-Lee wanted to connect data in many different ways so that a user could start from any point and move from topic to topic. He started working on a new program called Enquire. He began by creating a single page, called a node. To create another page, he had to come up with a way to link it to the first node. Every page had to be connected in some logical way to a previous page. The program stored information on how people, projects, and software were connected and made it possible for users to move between them in unique ways.

How Enquire Worked

Enquire was built using computer science tools that already existed. It relied on the Internet, which is now a global network and a part of daily life for billions of people around the world. When Berners-Lee first developed Enquire, the Internet was used by government agencies, universities, some big corporations, and institutions such as CERN.

During the 1970s, the U.S. government developed the Internet as a way to allow data to be transmitted between computers over telephone wires through a system of servers and nodes. Each computer represented a node in the network, and the nodes were connected to a central computer called a server.

Networks could be very big, or they could be made up of just two or three computers. There was not a way for different networks to communicate with one another. Berners-Lee's program made it possi-

PROJECT XANADU

Berners-Lee's Enquire program was not the first computer software to use hypertext. In 1960, a graduate student named Ted Nelson in the Sociology Department at Harvard University came up with an idea for a computer program that would allow users to easily edit, revise, compare, and delete their work. It would be a global publishing tool, a library, and a place where discussions and debates about ideas could take place. He called it Project Xanadu and began working on it that year. In the years that followed, he invented the concept of using text to link electronic documents to each other. He coined the phrase "hypertext" to describe these links. He and a team of assistants built a demonstration model in 1974, but it took Nelson until 2014 to finish a working model. Nelson's project never became the universal library that he envisioned, but his pioneering work and his hypertext concept inspired many other programmers and tech innovators.

ble through the use of hypertext links—which were still a relatively new idea. Hypertext is text—words or phrases—that is displayed on a computer and is programmed with references (called hyperlinks) that allow users to immediately access other text.

Berners-Lee never published Enquire, which only worked on the type of computers he used at CERN. However, it worked very well. The connection-based design let him access information quickly and easily. When he left his consulting job there in December 1980, he gave a copy of the program—written on an eight-inch floppy disc—to an assistant manager at CERN.

CONSULTING

Berners-Lee and Rogers left CERN at the end of 1980 and returned to England to work for a company called Image Computer Systems. The company was operated by their friend and former employer John Poole. Poole wanted them to help design software. Berners-Lee took charge of several important projects, many of them relating to software for state-of-the-art printers. He built graphics and communication software. Poole was happy to bring him back. He appreciated Berners-Lee's intelligence, his easy-going nature, and his determination.

Berners-Lee stayed at the company for about three years. He worked on the company's computer networks, created programs that streamlined the printing process, and contributed to several other Image projects. In his spare time, he continued to think about Enquire and what could happen if he found a way to create a space where many types of computers and machines could connect to one another.

RETURN TO CERN

Berners-Lee had enjoyed his time at CERN, and in 1984 he was offered a fellowship at the institution. He

Early personal computers, such as this Acorn model from 1984, were far too expensive for most people to have at home at that time.

received strong recommendations from Poole and several of his colleagues at Image. Poole gave him credit for much of Image's growth. When Berners-Lee left the company in September 1984, Poole gave him a personal computer (PC). Companies had just started making PCs for the public, and they were bulky and expensive by today's standards, but they could at least be easily moved from place to place. Berners-Lee was happy to have his very own portable computer that he could take to Switzerland.

Chapter Three

Communication Reimagined

Berners-Lee encountered problems with organizing information at CERN. At the time, the laboratory was the largest Internet node in the world. Berners-Lee saw the organizational problems as an opportunity to connect hypertext with computer networking principles to create a new kind of network.

FASTBUS AND CERNDOC

He joined a team that was designing a computer system for the laboratory's new particle accelerator. The program, called FASTBUS, was intended to help other computers in the CERN network collect data from experiments so that scientists could study atomic particles. He also began thinking about another computer system called CERNDOC, which was used to store documents and data. CERNDOC was engineered in the classic hierarchical structure. Berners-Lee thought that his Enquire program would make it easier for users to find the information they wanted. He wrote a new version of Enquire and started working out how he could apply it to CERNDOC.

Enquire worked only on individual computers. He wanted to be able to run it on many computers at one time and have them communicate with one another. One of his assignments was to develop computer codes called Remote Procedure Call that would let one computer tell another what to do. He liked the project, but it wouldn't let researchers share their data across the many systems at CERN. He decided to experiment with using the Internet to share information.

THE HYPERTEXT PLAN

Berners-Lee used hypertext in both versions of his Enquire program. He thought he could combine it with the Internet to create a system that would allow him easily to look up and cross-reference information. Computer users would follow highlighted hypertext links from one page to other pages, regardless of what kind of computer or network stored the page. People across departments at CERN would be able to look at the same data without having to spend time re-copying it.

For his plan to work, he needed to change the way networks were usually built. Instead of having a central computer act as the hub where all the documents and data would be stored, information would be transferred directly from one computer to another. Documents could be stored on computers located anywhere, and people would be able to access them no matter where the computer was located.

THE EARLY INTERNET

Berners-Lee's idea relied on using the Internet, which was first proposed in 1960 by American psychologist and computer scientist Joseph Carl Robnett Licklider (1915–1990). In 1962, Licklider was hired by the U.S. Department of Defense to lead the Information Techniques Processing Office within the Defense Advanced Research Projects Agency (DARPA) and to find a way to connect the department's main computers to each other. The project resulted in an early network called the Advanced Research Projects Agency Network (ARPANET), which was completed in 1969.

The early Internet was refined throughout the 1970s, as more branches of government and universities developed their own networks. Information could be shared between computers, but the variety of machines available sometimes made it difficult. More companies were

Computer scientist Joseph Carl Robnett Licklider is seen here with one of his students. Licklider predicted that the Internet would change the distribution of music and media.

building computers in the late 1970s and early 1980s, and the variety meant that different kinds of computers often were not able to communicate with one another through a network.

CREATING THE WORLD WIDE WEB

Berners-Lee was thrilled with his idea for combining hypertext with the Internet, but he would need far more time to work on the project. Unlike Enquire, it was too big to build in his spare time. In March 1989, he wrote up a formal proposal and gave it to his boss, Mike Sendall. He explained that he wanted to combine hypertext with two of the foundations of the Internet--the Domain Name System (DNS) and Transmission Control Protocol (TCP).

Domain names are the familiar, easy-to-memorize names for websites. The Domain Name System translates these domain names into a code called Internet Protocol (IP), which tells a computer how to locate and communicate with another computer over the Internet. Every computer and device with an Internet connection has an IP address. The DNS did not exist when Berners-Lee wrote the first version of Enquire. The DNS was designed in 1983 by two computer scientists named Paul Mockapetris and Jon Postel at the University of California, Irvine.

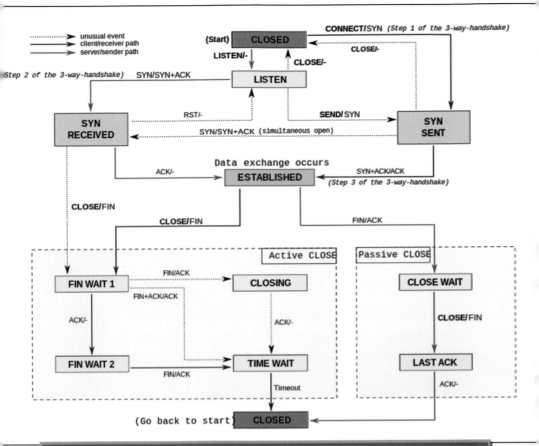

A diagram shows the way computers use Transmission Control Protocol to send and receive data while establishing a network connection and then disconnecting.

Transmission Control Protocol is a computer code for transmitting data between computers. It was invented in 1974 to solve the problem of computer networks not being able to communicate with one another. TCP became the standard for establishing a connection and exchanging data and helped the Internet grow into a network of networks.

BUILDING BLOCKS OF ARPANET

ARPANET used two technologies that became the foundation of the Internet: packet switching and the Transmission Control Protocol and Internet Protocol (TCP/IP) suite. In packet switching, data stored on one computer is divided into blocks called packets, which are transmitted through networks and then reassembled so that they can be viewed on another computer. The four university computers that were part of the first ARPANET network were in turn connected to gateway computers called Interface Message Processors (IMPs). The IMPs divided each message into packets for transmission and put the packets back together to receive information. ARPANET later used Transmission Control Protocol to enable communication with other computer networks.

Berners-Lee called his new version of Enquire "Tangle." He thought that if he could use hypertext, the DNS, and TCP to bring Tangle to the Internet, he could provide a great service to the scientists at CERN. It wouldn't matter what kind of computers they were using because all the machines would be able to access the Internet documents, so long as they were connected by hypertext links.

Berners-Lee explained his plan in a paper he wrote in March 1989 titled "Information Management: A Proposal" and applied for a grant from CERN to develop the concept. At first, Sendall didn't fully understand the proposal, but he saw Berners-Lee's enthusiasm for the idea and sensed that it had great potential. He agreed to send the proposal along to other decision makers at CERN who were responsible for deciding which projects could be funded.

Berners-Lee's project was not directly related to physics. No one at CERN could authorize funding it or letting him use the equipment he needed to make his idea a reality. Some of his colleagues at CERN liked the project, but most were not interested. Berners-Lee was not discouraged and continued to learn about the Internet and hypertext while he waited for an official response to his proposal.

OFFLINE AT CERN

Berners-Lee was passionate about his work at CERN. His assignments and thinking about how to make his proposal work took up a lot of his time. Yet he found chances to step away from the lab and give himself breaks. He sang and acted in musicals staged by a local amateur theater group. Always interested in the outdoors, he went skiing in the Alps.

Scientists monitor a giant fanlike sensor at Fermilab's Tevatron particle accelerator in 1990. It was once the largest particle accelerator in the world.

He also met his second wife while at CERN. Nancy Carlson was a computer programmer from the United States and a former figure skater. She was working for the World Health Organization in Geneva at the same time Berners-Lee was at CERN for his fellowship. Like him, she spent some of her spare time working in amateur theatrical productions. They met after he saw her in one of her plays, and they soon began dating. They became engaged in 1989. That winter, he took his first trip to the United States with her and met her family in Connecticut. Tim and Nancy were married there in July 1990.

Berners-Lee used the trip to learn more about the building blocks of his project. He traveled to Fermilab—a physics laboratory located on the outskirts of Chicago, Illinois—to study the computer systems there. He also took a trip to Maryland to attend a workshop on hypertext. By the time he returned to CERN, Berners-Lee was certain that hypertext would be the key to making his project work.

Chapter Four

JUMP-STARTING THE WORLD WIDE WEB

Taking the World Wide Web from an idea in a paper to an online entity took a lot of hard work and planning on Berners-Lee's part, as well as the cooperation of CERN and the work of many scientists and engineers.

HITTING RESTART

When Tim and Nancy returned from the United States in 1990, he found out that researchers at the facility had gotten a new computer called the NeXT. Built by Apple cofounder Steve Jobs, the NeXT was a sleek and elegant machine. Inside its black plastic casing, Jobs had packaged a processor that was far more powerful than any other personal computer on the market.

Apple cofounder Steve Jobs started the NeXT computer company in 1985. A NeXT computer, such as the one Berners-Lee obtained, was powerful, but very expensive.

Berners-Lee decided that such a machine could help him develop his idea into reality. He requested one from Mike Sendall. Sendall arranged to order two of the little supercomputers and gave Berners-Lee permission to start working on his hypertext program. They did not yet have official approval from CERN management, but they expected the value of Berners-Lee's idea to become clear once it was put into action. Berners-Lee again sent out his proposal and waited for his computers to arrive.

Circulating the proposal a second time paid off. Berners-Lee's idea caught the attention of Belgian engineer and computer scientist Robert Cailliau. Berners-Lee and Cailliau had known each other briefly when both men worked at CERN in 1980, but they didn't cross paths again until Mike Sendall brought them together. Sendall realized that the two engineers had

similar ideas and suggested that they meet, and they quickly began working together. Their different personalities complemented each other well. Berners-Lee was casual about planning and scheduling, and he tended to concentrate on the broader parts of the project. Cailliau liked everything to be planned out ahead of time and was a master at getting small details just right.

CERN computer scientist Ben Segal, Tim Berners-Lee, and Robert Cailliau pose with the NeXT computer that was the world's first Web server.

Cailliau started by improving Berners-Lee's proposal. Berners-Lee had described the general idea well but had left out specifics about how the project would be managed. Cailliau added details such as a projected cost, how many people they would need, and a schedule for finishing the project. They submitted it to CERN with the formal title "World Wide Web: Proposal for a Hypertext Project."

Berners-Lee had considered several names for the project, including Information Mesh and Information Mine. He thought "mesh" sounded too much like "mess" and didn't want people thinking about his project in that way. Information Mine was closer, because he liked the image of people digging for information. However, the initials for "The Information Mine" could be taken to spell "TIM," and he didn't want people to think that he was naming it after himself. He chose "World Wide Web" because he liked the sound of it and it perfectly described his project as a global "web" of information.

ANOTHER FRUSTRATION

Once again, CERN did not give full approval for the proposed project. Berners-Lee and Cailliau realized that besides themselves and Sendall, very few of the scientists at CERN were interested. In the interim, Berners-Lee received his NeXT computer in the fall of 1990. He was officially supposed to be designing software for controlling particle accelerators, but there were not any experiments going on at that time because the facility was waiting for its new accelerator to open. With his powerful new computer and Cailliau alongside him to help him with the organization, Berners-Lee started working on making the Web a reality.

BUILDING THE INFRASTRUCTURE

Berners-Lee wanted the World Wide Web to be the sort of tool that would be easy for anyone to use, not just a specialized program for engineers and computer scientists. He envisioned a Web that would let people use hypertext to create pages. These pages would include highlighted words or phrases that would serve as links to more pages. The user could keep following links through the Web, gaining deeper knowledge all the time.

Berners-Lee developed a tool called hypertext transfer protocol (HTTP) for use in retrieving information over the Internet and transmitting hypertext. Computers communicated with each other through hypertext. HTTP allowed one section of a document to be electronically linked to another part of the same document. To get there, the user clicks on the highlighted link and the screen goes to that part of the document. Transmitting hypertext was an entirely new idea. By adding new instructions to the Internet, Berners-Lee could expand it from a set of networks that existed as separate entities into an accessible web of information.

Berners-Lee needed to come up with a way for computers to find the Web page that the user wanted. He decided that each page would have an address that would tell the computer where it could be found. These addresses were called Universal Document Identifiers (UDIs), though the name was later changed to Uniform Resource Locators (URLs).

BREAKING DOWN A URL

A URL tells the browser which directories to use to find that specific site. The first part tells the browser what type of resource it is looking for—http for a hypertext page or directory, for example—and is separated from the rest by a colon and two forward slashes. It is often unnecessary to type this part of the URL. The second part contains the address of the computer that stores the document. In the URL http://home.web.cern.ch/topics/birth-web, for example, the "home.web.cern.ch" part is the address of the host computer, while "/topics/birth-web" is the pathway to the actual file.

Berners-Lee set up a network system for his World Wide Web project. The software that stores all the location data was housed on powerful computers with a lot of memory space. They would act as Web servers. His NeXT computer at CERN was the world's first Web server. Other computers that connected to the Web would be called Web clients. These can include desktop personal computers or any Internet-ready device, such as a smartphone or tablet. They are the means by which people access the World Wide Web. People can also store pages on these machines and make them accessible to the public via the Web.

The First Browser

The network principle behind the World Wide Web lacked one element: an easy way for people to access the pages stored on other computers. Berners-Lee's solution was to build a new software program called a browser. The browser, which he named WorldWideWeb, allowed users to view pages stored on other computers.

Berners-Lee recruited a small team to help with the project. It included a mathematics student at Leicester Polytechnic (now De Montfort University) named Nicola Pellow. She was assigned to help develop the browser. Pellow came to CERN as an intern and soon found herself in the middle of Berners-Lee's project.

Another assistant, Jean-Francois Groff, helped him build a directory of Web addresses.

The basic format of that first browser is the same as with browsers today. A user first types in the URL of the website he or she wants, clicks on a hypertext link, or selects a bookmark. The browser identifies the Web page through a directory of IP addresses stored on the server and brings it up for the user.

One of the major obtacles Berners-Lee had to overcome was the problem that had started the entire project. He had to find a way to enable communication between various computer languages. Different types of computers were programmed in specific ways that often were not compatible with other machines. A Web client would not be able to access a page located on a Web server that was programmed in a different code.

INVENTING HTML

Berners-Lee decided that he would sidestep that problem by writing an entirely new computer language. He called it Hypertext Markup Language (HTML). It was based on hypertext, which he had been studying for years. Berners-Lee thought that HTML could serve as a common

Early Web pages were revolutionary for their graphics, such as the World Wide Web logo seen here, and links, all of which were made possible by Berners-Lee's HTML.

53

language that all computers could read using browser software. He was right, and even today HTML is the standard language used on the Web.

HTML acts as a set of instructions for interactions between client and server computers. The client computer requests a document through a browser. The server computer reads this request in HTML. The HTML gives the server directions for finding the document—which is located on another client computer—and the server can then send the document back to the first client computer to be displayed on the screen. Both client computers are nodes, and they could be located next to each other or thousands of miles away. The HTML can tell the browser to send the document wherever it is needed.

When the requested information comes back to the Web client computer that made the request, it is formatted in HTML. The browser translates the HTML into the text, colors, graphics, and images that make up a Web page. Hypertext links to other Web pages are also embedded in the document, enabling the user to truly explore a "web" of information.

Berners-Lee and his team worked quickly to build the computer codes they needed for the project. In just a few months, he had finished the initial work. He put the first Web client and Web server on his NeXT computer and passed out the software for reading and writing HTML to all the CERN scientists who had NeXT machines. On December 25, 1990, the World Wide Web officially went live. The whole Web at the time was contained on Berners-Lee's own NeXT computer, but it was a significant step.

Berners-Lee's personal life was also changing. On December 31, 1990, just a week after the Web went live, his wife gave birth to the couple's first child. They named the baby girl Alice. As focused as he could be on working on the Web and other projects at CERN, Berners-Lee was even more devoted to helping raise his daughter.

Building a Web Page

After taking some time off for Alice's birth, Berners-Lee returned to CERN to continue working on his project. Once the Web was up and running, he had to figure out what to do with it. He had developed the project at CERN and he wanted it to be useful to the scientists who worked at the facility, but he also hoped it could spread to other places, such as universities and other research centers. He dreamed of a time when the World Wide Web could be used by anyone.

To make that happen, Berners-Lee had to convince people at CERN to use the Web. Many thought the project was interesting, but they didn't believe it would be useful. He and Cailliau decided to use CERN's size and the vast number of people working there to generate interest.

Keeping track of all the scientists, researchers, interns, and institutions that were connected with CERN was an enormous task. The facility relied on phone books to stay in contact with these people and places, but the contact information was always changing. Berners-Lee decided that posting a master phone book on the Web would make it easy to access and update the phone numbers.

http://info.cern.ch/hypertext/WWW/T

World Wide Web

The WorldWideWeb (W3) is a wide-area hypermedia

Everything there is online about W3 is linked directly
Frequently Asked Questions .

What's out there?
Pointers to the world's online information, subj

Help
on the browser you are using

Software Products
A list of W3 project components and their curr

Technical
Details of protocols, formats, program interna

Bibliography
Paper documentation on W3 and references.

People
A list of some people involved in the project

RESTORING THE FIRST WEB PAGE

The first website was very simple by today's standards. It was little more than a list of links to information about the World Wide Web and how people could get involved in the project. In the next few years, the Internet grew to its current massive scale, and that first simple page on CERN's server disappeared. In 2013, CERN used archived copies to re-create a 1992 version of that original website and bring it back online. Users can click on a "WWW People" link to learn a little about the early backgrounds of Berners-Lee, Cailliau, Pellow, and others who worked on the project. Other links take users to lists of servers, technical information, and links to online resources that were available at the time. It offers a fascinating look at just how small the Web was in 1992.

The restoration of CERN's first Web page demonstrates Berners-Lee's desire to create a simple way to navigate the information that was available on the World Wide Web.

The directory project took a lot of work. The entire World Wide Web was still on Berners-Lee's NeXT computer. He and his team had to create a server that would work on CERN's central computer, where the contact information was stored. He recruited a computer programmer named Bernd Pollermann to help him complete the project. Pollermann helped maintain the central computer and knew how it worked. With his assistance, the Web server that Berners-Lee built for the central computer was able to access the phone numbers of everyone who worked at CERN. It could also supply Web pages containing that information. Berners-Lee taught Pollermann HTML so that he could build these Web pages. The directory became the first website.

The big problem that Berners-Lee faced was the question of how to give Web browsers to all of the scientists at CERN and how to make the browsers work on all of their different computers. Cailliau and Nicola Pellow played very important roles in creating browsers that could work across platforms. The WorldWideWeb browser that Tim built worked on CERN's NeXT computers, but it wasn't compatible with other computers.

Pellow was assigned the job of writing a very simple type of browser called the Line Mode Browser. This browser, which was referred to as a "passive browser," consisted only of text. There were no images or graphics, and it displayed only a black screen and green text. It was designed to be so basic that it could run on most computers that were available at that time.

It was very different from the browsers that are available today, or even from the WorldWideWeb browser. The user typed in a URL, and the browser would then print the corresponding Web page on the screen, line by line. Unlike Berners-Lee's WorldWideWeb browser, users couldn't navigate around on the page with a mouse or arrow keys. They had to type in text commands. The program also interpreted hypertext links as numbers, and users had to type those numbers into a command line to see those pages. The Line Mode Browser, which the team called WWW, was tested in December 1990 and was declared a success.

Within several months, Berners-Lee had demonstrated the system to researchers all over CERN, showing them how to access the Web and use the phone directory. At last, he was able to get the CERN scientists excited about his project. He and Pellow, Cailliau, and Pollermann visited with groups of researchers to explain how the Web could be used to exchange information. They kept giving demonstrations and handing out copies of the browsers.

Berners-Lee and Cailliau tried to make the Web more attractive by uploading more data on the server that Tim had set up on his NeXT computer. Scientists with the WorldWideWeb browser suddenly had more information to look at than just the directory. The browser also enabled them to create their own pages, which they could share with one another. This strategy worked for the small number of scientists who had NeXT computers, but most did not have these computers. These scientists were limited to using the Line Mode Browser, which did not let users write their own hypertext pages.

Chapter Five

THE ONLINE REVOLUTION

The World Wide Web existed for more than two years before most of the world knew about it. The project wasn't exactly a secret, particularly in the scientific communities that Berners-Lee was trying to recruit. However, only a small number of people owned computers at that time. Very few workers had access even to a local computer network within a company or organization. Smartphone technology was still more than a decade away. In 1991, Berners-Lee and his team started working to bring more attention to the World Wide Web. They wanted people around the world to use it and embrace its potential.

EXPANDING THE AUDIENCE

The World Wide Web project at CERN was still an underfunded novelty in 1991. Scientists were using the directory and some had started building Web pages, but it wasn't attracting the attention it needed to survive. Berners-Lee needed to win support for his project from scientists who were not associated with CERN. Working with his assistant, Jean-Francois Groff, Berners-Lee put together a code library called libWWW and made it available to the world. The library allowed programmers and computer enthusiasts to build their own browsers.

On August 6, 1991, Berners-Lee posted a message to the alt.hypertext newsgroup (an early form of message board) for NeXT computer users. In the post, Berners-Lee explained how the Internet could be used to distribute, share, and cross-reference documents around the world. He also made the World Wide Web software available to anyone with a NeXT computer, as well as a basic server that could be used by any computer, and a browser. More than one-half dozen browsers would be built over the next eighteen months, though Pellow's Line Mode Browser and his own WorldWideWeb browser remained the most commonly used ones.

He also reached out to other important people in the computer science world, such as Paul Kunz. Kunz was a physicist at Stanford University, in Palo Alto, California. He was active in the small community of people who used NeXT computers. At first, Kunz was not excited by the idea of the World Wide Web. He paid little attention to Berners-Lee's newsgroup posting and didn't even download the free code library. When he visited Europe that September, Kunz spent a few days touring the facilities at CERN. On the last day of his trip, September 13, Berners-Lee approached him and requested a meeting.

Kunz went along with Berners-Lee, though he was not very interested and was only being polite. He was unimpressed when Berners-Lee showed him how information retrieval worked between two NeXT computers. Berners-Lee then showed him how to use a browser to send a request for information from his NeXT computer to CERN's IBM mainframe. The two computers were not designed to interact with each other, but Berners-Lee was able to retrieve the information he wanted.

At that point, Kunz began to realize that Berners-Lee's World Wide Web idea had real value, but the two computers were still in the same building. Tim was then able to use the Internet to upload the browser software onto Kunz's computer, which was still in California. From CERN, they got the browser to work in California and sent a Web page to Kunz's computer, which then sent it back.

Stanford University physicist Paul Kunz created the first website in the United States. It consisted of three lines of text with links to e-mail and to a massive database.

Berners-Lee and the skeptical Kunz were impressed by how well their experiment worked. To get the Web page to bounce from Stanford to CERN, information had to travel across the Atlantic Ocean four times. Kunz left CERN the next day, and when he returned to Stanford he gave a demonstration by again connecting to CERN's Web servers. The demonstration went well, and the scientists and research staff there were impressed by the speed of the connection.

Kunz received permission from the Stanford Linear Accelerator Center's (SLAC) associate head librarian, Louise Addis, to make the university's collection of physics documents available over the World Wide Web. The university stored more than 300,000 physics documents and references on a database called the Stanford Public Information Retrieval System–High Energy Physics (SPIRES-HEP), but they were only accessible through the library computers. Addis understood that making the documents available to researchers all over the world could lead to major scientific breakthroughs.

Kunz built a Web server, and on December 12, 1991, he sent an e-mail to Berners-Lee and asked him to try it. A few minutes later, Berners-Lee responded with a note congratulating him. When the CERN and SLAC Web servers communicated with each other, the World

Tim Berners-Lee used this NeXT computer to build the World Wide Web. The machine also hosted the world's first Web server, "httpd."

Wide Web had finally become global.

Introducing the World Wide Web

One month after Kunz's successful Web server test, Berners-Lee spoke at a conference in France in front of more than two hundred physicists from around the world and demonstrated the World Wide Web application. At the end of his talk, he connected to the SLAC server and showed the audience how to do a SPIRES-HEP search. Instead of simply talking about an abstract idea for sharing information over interconnected computer networks, he gave the scientists a practical tool that excited them.

SPIRES-HEP became the first U.S. website and included a search tool created by Addis. By making

SPIRES-HEP's data instantly available from any connected computer, Kunz, Addis, and other scientists at Stanford built the breakthrough that inspired researchers to start using the World Wide Web.

NAVIGATING THE WEB

Early use of the World Wide Web was driven by researchers at CERN and SLAC. Soon, other institutions and scientists from disciplines other than physics started using the World Wide Web. Fermilab was one of the first facilities to join Stanford and CERN on the World Wide Web.

By the end of 1992, there were about twenty-six early websites and fifty servers at locations around the world. Most Web pages were serious and devoted to hard science, but there was some room for fun. Berners-Lee himself created a Web page for a band made up of CERN employees called Les Horribles Cernettes. He even included a picture of the all-female parody pop group, which became the first photo ever transmitted on the Web.

A team of young programmers at the Helsinki University of Technology in Finland created another browser called Erwise, while student Pei Wei at the University of California at Berkley built a browser called ViolaWWW. Both browsers worked on UNIX computers. Another team of CERN scientists built a browser called Samba, which worked on Macintosh computers. Berners-Lee was encouraged by all

THE MOSAIC REVOLUTION

The National Center for Supercomputing Applications (NCSA) at the University of Illinois at Urbana-Champaign was among the facilities that set up early servers. It was one of the main efforts by the U.S. government to encourage the development of the Web. Workers on the NCSA's server included a computer science student named Marc Andreessen. He and another NCSA worker named Eric Bina combined Berners-Lee's World Wide Web protocols with another early type of information retrieval system called Gopher to create a user-friendly browser called Mosaic that worked on many different types of computers and featured graphics. NCSA Mosaic was released in 1993 and is often credited with being the browser that popularized the World Wide Web. Berners-Lee tried Mosaic in February 1993 and found it very easy to use, although he worried that the graphics and colors would distract Web developers from the information-sharing goal of the Web.

these efforts, though none of these browsers allowed users to create their own Web pages. He hoped that this situation would change.

SETTING THE WEB FREE

Berners-Lee saw a potential problem with the number of browsers being introduced. He was concerned that certain browsers would not be able to access all the information on the Web. He didn't want a lot of specialized browsers that could access only certain pages or kinds of pages to fragment the Web, or for users to have to pay to access certain pages.

Forcing people to pay for accessing information could ruin the project, Berners-Lee believed. The early

Berners-Lee speaks to programmers gathered at the fourth international World Wide Web Conference in 1995. Attendees met to work together on technical standards.

information retrieval system called Gopher, built and operated by the University of Minnesota, had briefly competed with the World Wide Web for users. However, the university decided to charge people to use the browser and most people stopped using it.

Berners-Lee and Cailliau decided to take a drastic step to make sure that access to the Web would remain free. They convinced the leadership at CERN to make everything connected with the Web absolutely free. On April 30, 1993, they were notified that CERN would make the Web a public domain property, meaning that anyone would be free to use it to build a browser or put up a server without violating anyone's rights.

Chapter Six

THE EXPANDING WEB

Berners-Lee was thrilled with CERN's decision to make the Web public property, even though it meant he would never be able to profit directly from his invention. To him—and to the rest of the team—the World Wide Web project had always been about making it easier to find information, not making money. Two months later, he would have another reason to be happy. In June 1993, Nancy Berners-Lee gave birth to their son, Ben. Tim again took some time off to be with his family, but he never stopped thinking about what the Web would become and how he could help secure its future.

The year 1993 was a watershed year for the World Wide Web. Companies, government bodies, and educational institutions were getting involved. At last, the Web was taking off. Berners-Lee, however, saw a new potential problem. He worried that a company or a group might be able to control the Web by encouraging people to use a particular browser. He didn't want any one entity to be able to decide how people used the World Wide Web. He also worried about software being introduced to the Web without any sense of organization or standardization.

GUIDING PRINCIPLES OF THE WEB

Berners-Lee recommended that CERN create a governing body for the Web called a consortium, which would include businesses and government agencies and would be given the job of protecting the Web. Many of the businesses and institutions that were already connected to the Web had already asked for a central body to define the Web and help govern its growth. The consortium would make recommendations for how the Web could be improved, make it possible for the Web to smoothly adapt to new technology, and encourage people from all over the world to use it.

Berners-Lee presented his World Wide Web consortium idea to CERN in October 1993. He needed the support of a major organization to make his idea work, and CERN would be the perfect place to give his consortium a home. The research facility, however, was focused on other matters. Berners-Lee and Cailliau were actually the only CERN workers who were paid to work full-time on the Web.

Berners-Lee didn't hear from his superiors at CERN for several months. In the meantime, the Web was quickly growing beyond CERN's capabilities to support it. Marc Andreessen had started his own company, called Netscape, and was marketing browsers and servers. Several other companies, including Microsoft, were also either releasing or developing browsers. Companies were releasing competing versions of HTML that were not compatible with browsers designed by other firms.

In February 1994, Berners-Lee traveled to Brussels, Belgium, to meet with a computer science professor from the Massachusetts Institute of Technology (MIT) named Michael Dertouzos. He and Dertouzos had a similar vision for what the Web could become. They went over Berners-Lee's idea for a World Wide Web consortium and talked about the possibility of setting it up at MIT's Laboratory for Computer Science (MIT-LCS). They received support for what would become the World Wide Web Consortium (W3C) from DARPA and the European Commission, which is an organization of European governments and is now the decision-making governing body of the European Union.

It would be a huge step for Berners-Lee and his family. They loved their home in the French countryside,

Forming the World Wide Web Consortium brought Berners-Lee to the United States, where in 1998 he received a $270,000 MacArthur Fellowship for his pioneering work.

just outside of CERN. With the Alps nearby, Berners-Lee could hike and ski as he pleased. He and Nancy would have to leave their friends behind and move far from the place where they had been so happy. They would, however, be much closer to Nancy's family. Tim also recognized that use of the Web was more widespread in the United States than in Europe.

Many questions about how the consortium would be set up had to be answered. MIT would take the lead on the project, but Berners-Lee and Dertouzos both felt that it should have two headquarters, one in Massachusetts and the other at CERN. Finally, in May 1994, Berners-Lee agreed to head the W3 Consortium at MIT. That August, he and his family packed up their belongings in Europe, said good-bye to their friends, and headed off across the Atlantic Ocean to start a new life in Massachusetts.

A GROWING CONSORTIUM

The Berners-Lee family settled in Boston, and Tim started his new job as head of the World Wide Web Consortium on September 1, 1994. At that point, the consortium consisted of Tim, Michael Dertouzos, and another MIT computer science professor named Albert Vezza. They met often in those first few weeks to make plans and determine the consortium's direction.

They decided that they would establish some clear standards for HTML but that they would not in any way regulate who could create Web pages, how they would look, or what kind of information they contained. The consortium's advisory committee met for the first time that December, and Berners-Lee announced that the W3C would not have a central headquarters. Instead, it would be "hosted" at MIT and CERN, while branch offices would be established at other sites around the world. He also reinforced the idea of a free Web by saying that anyone would be able to build a browser and put up a server without getting permission from the consortium.

Membership would consist of willing nations, colleges and universities, research institutions, laboratories, businesses, corporations, and any other organization that wished to join. Organizations would have to apply to become members and would have to meet certain requirements. They would also have to pay annual dues to keep their membership, with the fees set to a sliding scale that depends on the type of organization applying and in which country it is located.

Soon after the advisory committee meeting, CERN informed Berners-Lee that it would not be able to participate in the consortium. The facility was devoting all its resources to its new supercollider project, and it would not have the money or personnel to spare for such a large side project. Berners-Lee was disappointed, but he quickly went to work on finding another European site.

The French Institute for Research in Computer Science and Automation (INRIA) in Paris volunteered to take CERN's place and in April 1995 became the consortium's European center. (It moved again to the European Research Consortium for Information and Mathematics [ERCIM], located in Sophia-Antipolis, France, in January 2003.) In 1996, the consortium opened a center at Keio University in Japan, just outside Tokyo. A fourth

Keio University was chosen to serve as a W3C host based on its reputation as one of Japan's leading computer science research centers and universities.

center located at Beihang University in Beijing, China, was announced in 2013.

Today, W3C has about 382 members, including from major corporations such as Apple and Google, social media sites such as Facebook, and government institutions such as the Library of Congress. Administrative duties, such as deciding where funds should be spent, are handled by a small administrative staff of about eighty people based at the four centers and led by a director and a chief executive officer. Berners-Lee

A WEB OF ACHIEVEMENTS

Tim Berners-Lee has been honored numerous times for his work in creating the World Wide Web. In 1999, *Time* named him as one of the "Time 100" greatest minds of the twentieth century. In 2004, he was knighted by Queen Elizabeth II for his "services to the global development of the Internet," according to his biography page on the W3C website. Other honors have followed. In June 2007, Queen Elizabeth II made him a member of a distinguished group called the Order of Merit. The order honors important contributions in the armed forces, art, literature, the promotion of culture, and science. Berners-Lee became one of only twenty-four living recipients, alongside such figures as the conductor Simon Rattle, playwright Tom Stoppard, and naturalist David Attenborough. He is also a Fellow of the Royal Society of Arts and the Royal Academy of Engineering.

In 2013, Berners-Lee became one of the first recipients of the Queen Elizabeth Prize for Engineering from Queen Elizabeth II in a ceremony held at Buckingham Palace.

has been the director since 1994. As of May 2015, the consortium also has offices in eighteen countries and on every continent except Antarctica.

The members decide rules, policies, and responsibilities. Each member organization has one representative on the Advisory Committee. This committee elects members to serve in a number of smaller, specialized committees. These include the Advisory Board elected from the Advisory Committee members and the Technical Architecture Group, which documents the principles for how the Web is structured. The director and the CEO decide when agreement has been reached on a needed change. Chartered groups made up of member representatives and invited guests make the changes that the members decide are needed.

RETURNING TO RELIGION

While Berners-Lee was working on starting the consortium, he was also going through some personal changes. He had been raised as a member of the Church of England, a Protestant Christian denomination, but he had turned away from the faith when he was a teenager. He simply felt that the church asked him to believe in too many things that he found unbelievable.

After they became parents, Tim and Nancy decided that they wanted their children to have a spiritual upbringing. They wanted their children to respect people of different faiths, but they didn't want them to be restricted in any way by religious teachings. Shortly after their move to Boston, they started attending a Unitarian Universalist church.

The Unitarian religion encourages people to take their own spiritual path. Instead of asking followers to accept specific teachings, the faith asks that they follow a set of seven guiding principles that recognize the value and dignity of others and the importance of acceptance and respect. Berners-Lee has written that he was drawn to the church's teachings of tolerance and acceptance. He remains very active in the Unitarian Universalist community.

Chapter Seven

An Online Legacy

The World Wide Web has grown and changed significantly since Berners-Lee became head of the W3C. When Berners-Lee first released the World Wide Web, the only people who knew anything about it or used it were scientists, researchers, and other academics. Most people who worked with computers used them only at their jobs. PCs were considered very expensive, and many people couldn't afford them. Eventually, PCs dropped in price. People could afford to buy them for their homes. They started finding out about the Web and connecting.

A Connected World

About 16 million people worldwide were using the World Wide Web in December 1995, according to the International

Data Corporation. By that time in 1996, the number of Web users had shot up to 36 million as companies realized that they could reach more customers by setting up public websites and selling products online.

By December 2000, about 361 million people were using the Web, according to Internet World Stats (IWS). The number crossed the one billion–user mark in December 2005 and continued to grow. IWS found that 2.8 billion people were using the Web in December 2013 and crossed the 3 billion mark in June 2014 out of a total world population of slightly more than 7 billion.

More had changed than just the incredible growth of Web usage. The ways in which people accessed the World Wide Web were also changing. In the early days, computers could access the Internet and the Web only by using dial-up modems that that could communicate at 56 kilobytes per second at their fastest. Networking technology evolved and the dial-up modems were mostly replaced by Ethernet and Digital Subscriber Line (DSL) connections, while broadband Internet service enabled faster transmission speeds than ever before.

Refined wireless technology made it possible to connect to the Internet and use the Web without cables. Hardware companies such as Apple and Microsoft began making smartphones, tablets, and other highly portable mobile devices that could connect to the Web from any location, provided they could pick up a signal. Today,

Tim Berners-Lee's invention is accessible from all but the most remote places in the world.

The way the World Wide Web looks has also changed, thanks to evolving technology. Computer processing power evolved to the point where PCs could transmit and receive sharp graphics, large music files, and videos. Faster connections made it possible and practical to share these large files through the World Wide Web. People can use the Web to watch movies, listen to music, and make phone calls. The World Wide Web has entered daily life to the point that people use it to pay bills, shop, file their tax returns, and even order food from local

The invention of the World Wide Web and improvements to computer technology make it possible for students to use tablets in the classroom.

restaurants. All these changes have their foundation in Berners-Lee's work.

REFINING THE WEB

Berners-Lee remains a very active presence in shaping the Web through his work with W3C, and he continues to work on Web-related projects. In 2004, he joined the faculty of the University of Southampton's School of Electronics and Computer Science to work on a new project called the Semantic Web. With this project, he envisioned a web of data that could be combined and used in many different ways. He expected the Semantic Web to be the next point in the World Wide Web's evolution, but that expectation has largely gone unrealized.

Berners-Lee remains committed to keeping the Web free and as accessible as possible. He opposes efforts to monitor Web traffic and other communications.

In 2009, he joined with an artificial intelligence expert named Nigel Shadbolt to establish the Open Data Institute (ODI). Based in London, the institute's purpose is to provide training in open data, the idea that certain information should be available for anyone to use or publish, to support such projects. It also aims to increase government transparency, so that ordinary citizens would be able to see how their government is run and its programs funded. He and Shadbolt led a project called data .go.uk, which was an effort by the United Kingdom to make non-personal data that was gathered by the government available to the public. In 2010, the ODI succeeded in bringing British government land survey data online, a step that Tim felt was important to making data more open. Berners-Lee became the ODI's president in 2012.

In addition to his work with the ODI and his responsibilities at MIT,

Tim has worked hard in recent years to improve access to the World Wide Web. He established the World Wide Web Foundation in November 2009 with the goal of improving the Web itself. The group's main goal is to help people use the Web to bring about positive change. The group also works toward the goal of making sure everyone can access the Web and use it freely.

Berners-Lee (*second from right*), his wife Rosemary Leith (*third from right*), and his children attend the 2014 Webby Awards, which honor excellence on the Internet.

87

While Berners-Lee was focusing more energy on these projects, his family life was undergoing major changes. Tim and Nancy Berners-Lee decided to end their marriage in 2011. At that point, their two children were nearly grown. Soon after the couple divorced, Tim started dating a woman named Rosemary Leith. She was one of the founding directors of the World Wide Web Foundation and a Fellow at Harvard University's Berkman Center for Internet & Society. They had known each other for years and worked together on many projects. They were married in June 2014.

In 2013, Berners-Lee helped launch the Alliance for Affordable Internet, which was set up to increase Internet availability in developing parts of the world. The organization is dedicated to making Internet access more affordable in the developing world. Berners-Lee and the other members of the alliance—including Microsoft, Google, and Facebook—work toward the goal of reducing the cost of a connection to less than 5 percent of a person's monthly earnings.

WEB OF THE FUTURE

Tim Berners-Lee has said that he sees the Web as a positive invention, although he never expected the commercial side of it to take off as it did. He also has said that he is not sorry that he did not patent the World Wide Web, even though he

THE NET NEUTRALITY DEBATE

Net neutrality is the idea that all Internet traffic should be treated equally by service providers. This includes sites on the World Wide Web. Until recently, the United States did not have any laws protecting Internet traffic. This lapse meant that Internet service providers could treat individual customers and various types of data differently. In 2014, the Federal Communications Commission (FCC) faced the choice of either creating two levels of broadband Internet service—a very fast one for customers who could pay for it, and a much slower one for everyone else—or defining broadband Internet as a telecommunications service. Berners-Lee and many other Web innovators spoke out in favor of redefining broadband and therefore keeping net neutrality. They believed a two-tiered Web would stifle information sharing and creativity on the Web. In February 2015, the FCC decided to protect net neutrality.

could have become incredibly rich by owning the rights to his invention. His only regret on that subject is that if he had done so, he could have given more money to charities.

Berners-Lee expects the World Wide Web to keep growing and that devices will continue to become smaller and faster. Instead of the ability to connect and connection speeds, privacy and the increasing use of data in daily lives will be the factors that will shape how people interact with the Web.

However, he also believes that certain safeguards should be put into place as more and more personal data moves onto the Web. In a 2014 interview with the *London Evening Standard*, Berners-Lee said that better security is needed to protect vital information. He also said that he feels that governments, companies,

Berners-Lee speaks at a press conference on human rights with officials from the United Nations. Access to the World Wide Web remains one of his top concerns.

ir Tim Berners-Lee

and groups should be more open and transparent about how personal data is used. He believes that the Web should serve and reflect humanity, and that a system of checks and balances should be in place to prevent any one individual, group, company, or government from controlling it. He embraces the collection and storage of data made possible through cloud computing, but only if it is made useful to individuals and if people own their own data.

The growth of the Web and the evolution of the machines people use to access it—from his NeXT computer at CERN to the latest wearable technology—have brought many changes. Cloud computing—the use of programs and services offered over the Internet—is seen by many as the latest big step in the evolution of the Web. Its roots can still be traced back to an idea hatched by Tim Berners-Lee.

Timeline

June 8, 1955 Timothy John Berners-Lee is born in London, England.

1966 Tim enrolls at Emanuel School.

1973 He graduates from Emanuel School and enrolls at Oxford University.

1976 Tim Berners-Lee graduates from Oxford's Queen's College with high honors. He goes to work at Plessey Telecommunications and marries Jane Northcote.

1978 Berners-Lee leaves Plessey to work at D. G. Nash.

1979 He becomes an independent consultant.

June 1980 He goes to CERN to work as a consultant. He writes the first version of Enquire using hypertext.

1981 He goes to work at Image Computer Systems.

1984 He accepts a fellowship at CERN. John Poole gives Berners-Lee a personal computer.

March 1989 Berners-Lee first outlines the idea for the World Wide Web in a paper titled

"Information Management: A Proposal."

1989 He meets Nancy Carlson at CERN.

July 1990 He marries Carlson.

1990 He gets a NeXT computer at CERN. He teams up with Robert Cailliau to work on his proposal. The Line Mode Browser and the World Wide Web browser are created.

December 25, 1990 The World Wide Web goes live on Berners-Lee's NeXT computer.

December 31, 1990 Nancy Berners-Lee gives birth to their daughter.

1991 Berners-Lee creates an online directory for CERN.

August 6, 1991 He creates a post explaining the World Wide Web on the alt. hypertext newsgroup and makes Web software available.

September 13, 1991 Paul Kunz of Stanford University watches Berners-Lee demonstrate the Web.

December 12, 1991 Kunz connects his server at Stanford with CERN's server.

1992 The number of web servers passes fifty.

1993 The NCSA Mosaic browser is released.

April 30, 1993 CERN puts the World Wide Web in the public domain.

June 1993 Nancy and Tim's son, Ben, is born.

October 1993 Berners-Lee proposes the creation of the World Wide Web Consortium.

May 1994 He agrees to help establish and lead the W3C at the Massachusetts Institute of Technology.

August 1994 The Berners-Lee family moves to Massachusetts.

1999 Tim Berners-Lee is named one of the "Time 100" greatest minds of the twentieth century.

December 2000 More than 361 million people are connected through the World Wide Web.

2004 Berners-Lee is knighted by Queen Elizabeth II. He joins the faculty at the University of Southampton's School of Electronics and Computer Science.

2009 He joins with Nigel Shadbolt to establish the Open Data Institute. He creates the World Wide Web Foundation.

2011 Tim and Nancy Berners-Lee decide to end their marriage.

2012 Berners-Lee becomes president of the Open Data Institute.

2013 He launches the Alliance for Affordable Internet.

June 2014 He marries Rosemary Leith. More than three billion people are connected through the World Wide Web.

May 2015 The National Portrait Gallery in London unveils a painted bronze sculpture of Tim Berners-Lee by Sean Henry. Berners-Lee advises the British people to fight the government's plan to increase the country's surveillance powers and urges privacy protection.

Glossary

automate To use control systems to run machinery and mechanical processes.

browser A computer program that provides access to information through a network, especially access to websites.

compatible Able to exist and perform together in harmony.

computer science The branch of engineering that deals with computer hardware and software.

consortium A group of individuals, companies, or groups that agree to work together to reach a common goal.

consultant An individual who gives professional advice.

copyright The exclusive right to control intellectual property, such as a book or piece of music, for a certain period of time.

electromagnet A powerful magnet that uses an electric current passed in a wire around it to produce its force.

hierarchical Classified in layers, often from a large group to smaller groups.

hypertext A computer system that lets users move to new information by clicking on highlighted text.

infrastructure The basic features or structure of a system or organization.

mainframe A powerful computer that has smaller computers connected to it for individual users.

microchip A small piece of silicon that contains the electrical connections that make a computer work.

node A computer that is hooked up to a computer network.

nuclear physics The branch of physics that studies the makeup of atoms.

processor The part of a computer that performs and controls all of its operations.

program A series of instructions that makes a computer perform a certain task or action.

protocol A method for formalizing the way data is sent and received over the Internet.

public domain Property rights held by the public at large.

server A computer that controls or performs certain tasks for other computers in a network.

skeptical Having doubts about something that others believe is true or right.

software Programs used by computers for doing certain jobs.

For More Information

The Canadian Trade Commissioner Service
TCS Enquiries Service
Foreign Affairs and International Trade Canada
125 Sussex Drive
Ottawa, ON K1A 0G2
Canada
(888) 306-9991
Website: http://www.tradecommissioner.gc.ca
The Canadian Trade Commissioner Service helps
companies grow on a global scale by lowering the
cost of doing business.

CERN
Press Office
CH-1211 Geneva 23
Switzerland
Website: http://home.web.cern.ch
CERN is the European Organization for Nuclear
Research. Its scientists study the structure of the
universe. See http://home.web.cern.ch/topics/
birth-web for its online history of the World
Wide Web.

Computer History Museum
1401 North Shoreline Boulevard
Mountain View, CA 94043
(650) 810-1010
Website: http://www.computerhistory.org
The Computer History Museum preserves and pres-
ents artifacts and stories of the information age.

MediaSmarts—Canada's Center for Digital and
Media Literacy
950 Gladstone Avenue, Suite 120
Ottawa, ON K1Y 3E6
Canada
(800) 896-3342
Website: http://mediasmarts.ca
The website for this network contains a selection of
digital literacy resources for students, teachers,
and parents.

National Science Foundation (NSF)
4201 Wilson Boulevard
Arlington, VA 22230
(703) 292-5111
Website: http://www.nsf.gov

The NSF is a government agency that funds scientific research in a variety of fields. It has a Division of Computer and Network Systems and provides funding opportunities and programs for research and education.

The World Wide Web Consortium
W3C/MIT
32 Vassar Street, Room 32-G515
Cambridge, MA 02139
(617) 253-2613
Website: http://www.w3.org
The World Wide Web Consortium (W3C) is an international community where member organizations, a full-time staff, and the public work together to develop Web standards.

WEBSITES

Because of the changing nature of Internet links, Rosen Publishing has developed an online list of websites related to the subject of this book. This site is updated regularly. Please use this link to access the list:
http://www.rosenlinks.com/TP/Bern

For Further Reading

Anniss, Matt. *What Is a Website and How Do I Use It?* (Practical Technology). New York, NY: Britannica Educational Publishing and Rosen Educational Services, 2014.

Brasch, Nicholas. *The Internet* (The Technology Behind). Mankato, MN: Smart Apple Media, 2011.

Curley, Robert, ed. *Breakthroughs in Telephone Technology: From Bell to Smartphones* (Computing and Connecting in the 21st Century). New York, NY: Britannica Educational Publishing and Rosen Educational Services, 2012.

Curley, Robert, ed. *Computing: From the Abacus to the iPad* (Computing and Connecting in the 21st Century). New York, NY: Britannica Educational Publishing and Rosen Educational Services, 2012.

Duckett, Jon. *HTML and CSS: Design and Build Websites*. Indianapolis, IN: Wiley, 2014.

Espejo, Roman. *Policing the Internet* (At Issue). Detroit, MI: Greenhaven Press, 2012.

Foege, Alec. *The Tinkerers: The Amateurs, DIYers, and Inventors Who Make America Great*. New York, NY: Basic Books, 2013.

Furgang, Kathy. *Money-Making Opportunities for Teens Who Are Computer Savvy* (Make Money Now!). New York, NY: Rosen Publishing, 2014.

Goldsmith, Mike. *Computer* (DK Eyewitness Books). New York, NY: DK Publishing, 2011.

Hartman, Kate. *Make: Wearable Electronics*. Sebastopol, CA: Maker Media, 2014.

Harvey, Damian. *Tim Berners-Lee* (History Heroes). London, UK: Franklin Watts, 2014.

Henderson, Harry. *The Digital Age*. San Diego, CA: ReferencePoint Books, 2013.

Jackson, Tom. *The Basics of Atoms and Molocules* (Core Concepts). New York, NY: Rosen Publishing, 2014.

Kallen, Stuart A. *The Information Revolution* (World History). Detroit, MI: Lucent Books, 2011.

Karam, P. Andrew. *Artificial Intelligence* (Science Foundations). New York, NY: Chelsea House Publishers, 2012.

Karvinen, Tero, Kimmo Karvinen, and Ville Valtokari. *Make: Sensors*. Sebastopol, CA: Maker Media, 2014.

LaBerta, Catherine. *Computers Are Your Future*. Boston, MA: Pearson Prentice Hall, 2011.

Lapsley, Phil. *Exploding the Phone: The Untold Story of the Teenage Hackers and Outlaws Who Hacked Ma Bell*. New York, NY: Grove Press, 2014.

Marcovitz, Hal. *Online Information and Research*. San Diego, CA: ReferencePoint Press, 2012.

Marji, Majed. *Learn to Program with Scratch: A*

Visual Introduction to Programming with Art, Science, Math and Games. San Francisco, CA: No Starch Press, 2014.

Padua, Sydney. *The Thrilling Adventures of Lovelace and Babbage: The (Mostly) True Story of the First Computer*. New York, NY: Pantheon Books, 2015.

Pickover, Clifford A. *The Physics Book: From the Big Bang to Quantum Resurrection, 250 Milestones in the History of Physics*. New York, NY: Sterling Publishing, 2011.

Swanson, Jennifer A. *The Wonderful World of Wearable Devices* (Digital and Information Literacy). New York, NY: Rosen Publishing, 2015.

Szumski, Bonnie. *How Are Online Activities Affecting Society?* (In Controversy). San Diego, CA: ReferencePoint Press, 2013.

Walker, Pam, and Elaine Wood. *Computer Science Experiments*. New York, NY: Facts On File, 2010.

Wilkinson, Colin. *Going Live: Launching Your Digital Business* (Digital Entrepreneurship in the Age of Apps, the Web, and Mobile Devices). New York, NY: Rosen Publishing, 2013.

Willard, Nancy E. *Cyber Savvy: Embracing Digital Safety and Civility*. Thousand Oaks, CA: Corwin, 2012.

Bibliography

Abbate, Janet. "Oral History: Mary Lee Berners-Lee." *Institute of Electrical and Electronic Engineers*, September 12, 2001. Retrieved March 25, 2015 (http://ethw.org/Oral-History:Mary_Lee_Berners-Lee).

Academy of Achievement. "Interview: Timothy Berners-Lee, Father of the World Wide Web." June 22, 2007. Retrieved February 22, 2015 (http://www.achievement.org/autodoc/page/ber1int-1).

Albanesius, Chloe. "First Website Restored for 20th Anniversary of Open Web." *PC Magazine*, April 30, 2013. Retrieved April 20, 2015 (http://www.pcmag.com/article2/0,2817,2418330,00.asp).

Babbage Science and Technology. "The Q&A: Tim Berners-Lee: This Is for Everyone." *Economist*, September 5, 2012. Retrieved April 15, 2015 (http://www.economist.com/blogs/babbage/2012/09/qa-tim-berners-lee).

Berners-Lee, Tim. "Tim Berners-Lee on the Web at 25: The Past, Present, and Future." *Wired UK*, February 6, 2014. Retrieved March 3, 2015 (http://www.wired.co.uk/magazine/archive/2014/03/web-at-25/tim-berners-lee).

Berners-Lee, Tim, and Mark Fischetti. *Weaving the Web: The Original Design and Ultimate Destiny of the World Wide Web by Its Inventor.* New York, NY:

HarperCollins, 1999.

Gillies, James, and Robert Cailliau. *How the Web Was Born: The Story of the World Wide Web*. New York, NY: Oxford University Press, 2000.

Godwin, Richard. "People Will Always Try to Control the Internet. We Have to Keep Fighting for It." *London Evening Standard*, September 26, 2014. Retrieved March 15, 2015 (http://www.standard.co.uk/lifestyle/london-life/tim-bernerslee-some-people-will-always-try-to-control-the-internet-we-have-to-keep-fighting-for-it-9757371.html).

Greenemeier, Larry. "Remembering the Day the World Wide Web Was Born." *Scientific American*, March 12, 2009. Retrieved March 26, 2015 (http://www.scientificamerican.com/article/day-the-web-was-born/).

Hern, Alex. "Sir Tim Berners-Lee Speaks Out on Data Ownership." *Guardian*, October 8, 2014. Retrieved May 1, 2015 (http://www.theguardian.com/technology/2014/oct/08/sir-tim-berners-lee-speaks-out-on-data-ownership).

Internet Hall of Fame. "Tim Berners-Lee." Retrieved February 2, 2015 (http://internethalloffame.org/inductees/tim-berners-lee).

Internet World Stats. "And the 'Global Village' Became a Reality." Retrieved April 21, 2015 (http://www.internetworldstats.com/emarketing.htm).

Lasar, Matthew. "Before Netscape: The Forgotten Web

Browsers of the Early 1990s." *Ars Technica*, October 11, 2011. Retrieved May 1, 2015 (http://arstechnica.com/business/2011/10/before-netscape-forgotten-web-browsers-of-the-early-1990s).

Levy, Dawn. "Tech Pioneer Recalls How He Brought the World Wide Web, Now 10, to America." *Stanford Report*, December 12, 2001. Retrieved May 5, 2015 (http://news.stanford.edu/news/2001/december12/webturns10-1212.html).

Lytton, Charlotte, and Urmee Khan. "The Father of the Web Predicts Its Next Phase." CNN, December 23, 2014. Retrieved March 15, 2015 (http://www.cnn.com/2014/12/23/business/tim-berners-lee-future-insights/).

Metz, Cade. "Berners-Lee: World Finally Realizes Web Belongs to No One." *Wired*, June 6, 2012. Retrieved March 3, 2015 (http://www.wired.com/2012/06/sir-tim-berners-lee/).

New, William. "A Global Digital Magna Carta? Maybe, But First Identify Needs, Panel Says." Intellectual Property Watch, April 13, 2015. Retrieved May 1, 2015 (http://www.ip-watch.org/2015/04/13/a-global-digital-magna-carta-maybe-but-first-identify-what-is-needed-panel-says/).

New York Times. "Nancy Carlson Is Wed to Timothy Berners-Lee." July 15, 1990. Retrieved April 29, 2015 (http://www.nytimes.com/1990/07/15/style/nancy-carlson-is-wed-to-timothy-berners-lee.html).

Segaller, Stephen. *Nerds 2.0.1: A Brief History of the Internet*. New York, NY: TV Books, 1999.

Shankland, Stephen. "Tim Berners-Lee: 25 Years On, the Web Still Needs Work." CNET, March 11, 2014. Retrieved March 5, 2015 (http://www.cnet.com/news/tim-berners-lee-on-its-25th-anniversary-the-web-still-needs-work-q-a/).

Wired. "Top 12 Answers from Sir Tim Berners-Lee's Reddit AMA." Retrieved April 26, 2015 (http://www.wired.com/2015/03/top-12-answers-sir-tim-berners-lees-reddit-ama/).

Wolf, David. "The Curse of Xanadu." *Wired*, June 1995. Retrieved March 30, 2015 (http://archive.wired.com/wired/archive/3.06/xanadu.html).

World Wide Web Consortium. "Tim Berners-Lee Biography." Retrieved March 3, 2015 (http://www.w3.org/People/Berners-Lee/).

World Wide Web Foundation. "Tim Berners-Lee Married Rosemary Leith." Retrieved May 5, 2015 (http://webfoundation.org/tim-berners-lee-married-rosemary-leith/).

Wright, Robert. "The Man Who Invented the Web." *Time*, June 24, 2001. Retrieved April 8, 2015 (http://content.time.com/time/magazine/article/0,9171,137689,00.html).

Index

A

Alliance for Affordable Internet, 88
Andreessen, Marc, 68, 73
Apple, 44, 45, 77, 82
ARPANET, 36, 40

B

Babbage, Charles, 11
Berners-Lee, Conway, 10, 12, 14
Berners-Lee, Tim
  awards and honors, 78
  college years, 16–21
  early life, 8, 12–16
  personal life, 23, 41, 43, 55, 71, 79–80, 88
  religion, 79–80
  work life, 21–33

C

Cailliau, Robert, 46–49, 55, 57–59, 70, 73
CERN, 21, 26–29, 31, 32, 40–41, 44, 46, 48, 51, 54, 57–59, 62, 67, 70–73, 75, 76
CERNDOC, 34–35
cloud computing, 91

D

Defense Advanced Research Projects Agency (DARPA), 36, 73
Dertouzos, Michael, 73, 74–75
D. G. Nash, 25
Domain Name System (DNS), 38, 40

E

early computers, 9–10, 11, 25
Enquire information retrieval system, 29–31, 38
European Research Consortium for Information and Mathematics (ERCIM), 76

F

Facebook, 77, 88
FASTBUS, 34
French Institute for Research in Computer Science and Automation (INRIA), 76

G

Google, 77, 88

About the Author

Jason Porterfield is a writer and journalist living in Chicago, Illinois. He writes about tech subjects for several publications. Some of his technology books include *Julian Assange and Wikileaks*, *Niklas Zennström and Skype*, *Angry Birds and Rovio Entertainment*, and *Conducting Basic and Advanced Searches*.

Photo Credits

Cover, pp. 1, 86-87 Brad Barket/Getty Images; pp. 4-5 John W. McDonough/Sports Illustrated/Getty Images; pp. 8-9 © Nick Higham/Alamy; pp. 12-13 © Daily Mail/Rex/Alamy; p. 17 Pawika Tongtavee/Shutterstock.com; pp. 18-19, 24, 26-27, 66 Science & Society Picture Library/Getty Images; pp. 22-23 Walter Nurnberg/SSPL/Getty Images; pp. 32-33 Manchester Daily Express/SSPL/Getty Images; p. 37 The Boston Globe/Getty Images; p. 39 Scil100/Wikimedia Commons/File:Tcp state diagram fixed new.svg/CC BY-SA 3.0; p. 42 Michael L. Abramson/The LIFE Image Collection/Getty Images; pp. 45, 64, 69, 74 © AP Images; pp. 46-47 Sebastian Derungs/AFP/Getty Images; pp. 52-53 Science and Society/SuperStock; pp. 56-57 Fabrice Coffrini/AFP/Getty Images; p. 77 JTB Photo/Universal Images Group/Getty Images; p. 78 AFP/Getty Images; p. 83 Phil Boorman/Cultura/Getty Images; pp. 84-85 Press Association/AP Images; p. 90 Anadolu Agency/Getty Images; cover and interior pages VikaSuh/Shutterstock.com (light rays), evryka23/iStock/Thinkstock (light grid), Kotkoa/iStock/Thinkstock (circuit)
Designer: Brian Garvey; Editor: Kathy Kuhtz Campbell; Photo Researcher: Karen Huang